Conundrum Kids™

Best Wishes!
November, 2014

Kristen Flores
Ian Xander
Alisa Griffis, Ph.D.

About the Authors

Dr. Alisa Griffis currently serves as an adjunct professor of education at Indiana Wesleyan University. She is certified in elementary education and additionally holds credentials in English, Health, and Administration. Her recent teaching and research in education include literacy, brain research in learning acquisition for youth, differentiated instruction, and working with learning styles. Dr. Griffis has worked extensively with parents and students to help develop youth to their fullest potentials.

Kristen Flores has spent her early career working for non-profit organizations as a job developer with low socioeconomic inner city youth. She understands the unique challenges that young people experience when coming from generational poverty backgrounds, and works to develop job skills including interviewing, morality training, harassment prevention, developing a strong work ethic, and the development of written resumes, cover letters, and thank you notes. Mrs. Flores believes that her skills were directly influenced at a young age by playing the Conundrums game.

Ian Xander is a college student who is specializing in Psychology. He is a certified lifeguard, is a lifeguard and CPR trainer and supervisor, and has his Emergency Medical Technician certification. He credits his awareness and ability to work well with others from playing Conundrums as a child.

Table of Contents

4

Introduction

The game Conundrum first began when we, as a family, needed something to do with the kids on long driving trips. I started asking my children questions designed to sop up some time and keep them occupied, and soon it became a game: The kids loved the mental challenges they were presented.

Ian and Kristen soon begged for more and more scenarios. Unfortunately, my brain was concentrating on driving and sometimes the well ran dry. As the months and years passed, I struggled for more and more original and thought-provoking challenges to toss out. This book solves the problems that parents sometimes have with coming up with fresh, new conundrums to toss out to their children. Conundrum Kids has over three hundred scenarios for parents and teachers to use.

After playing "Conundrum" in the car for many months, I noticed that my children began to use more thought-filled analytical choices in their everyday lives. They had learned the art of thinking through a situation. By offering many different scenarios in a game-like form, the children were able to vicariously examine different potential solutions and become more considerate, intentional thinkers.

Since I often created common life scenarios for my kids to think through and debate, my children were able to "pre-live" these experiences. Then, when the situation arose in real life – they were already prepared. Instead of having to begin the thinking process fresh, they were able to reach a faster conclusion and outcome since they'd already thought about a similar situation in the past.

When we got wild and crazy with our game, I was begged to toss out highly challenging scenarios; the children really got excited about trying to figure out what would be the very best methodology to solve the problem.

Interestingly, I didn't always know how to solve the problem myself when I asked the question. That wasn't the point. If I asked something like, "You're in the woods and a bear runs at you. What should you do?" and I wasn't really, truly sure of the correct thing to do, we'd still play the game and they'd come up with solutions. Then we'd look it up when we got home and find out the "real" answer. This modeled for them what people do when they don't know how to solve a problem. They may toss around potential solutions and brainstorm and use logic and reasoning to try to figure out the answer, but ultimately, they'll research the answer as well.

There was another surprising outcome to this game: I got to know my children's likes and dislikes, preferences and tastes, abilities and skills, and moral and ethical dispositions very well. I was able to shape and guide them gently after hearing what they had to say. One thing that I learned to do, however, was hold my tongue at the time we were playing Conundrums. I had to learn to listen, even if one or both of the kids was picking a bizarre or even potentially dangerous choice. I allowed them to debate it back and forth, and learned to say, "Why might that *not* work?" when they finally announced that they'd come to agreement on a scenario.

I realized that if I got "preachy" – the fun would leave the game. My goal was long-term learning, not short-term lecturing. Sometimes I let the kids sit on a bad answer and then in a few days or a week, I'd discuss an article I'd found on the Internet that talked about just that sort of thing. I could then use an argument from authority to make my point for me. This kept me the good guy and still enabled the children to have a decision-changing experience. Then I'd tuck that information away and a few months later, I'd come up with a "similar but different" conundrum to see if the kids would come up with a better decision than their original one. They invariably did.

By creating these conundrums, I was also able to celebrate and sigh with relief when I realized my kids could handle a potentially tricky situation well. This translated to non-dangerous but ethical decision-making on their parts. By having the children go through the intentional and out-loud process of thinking through and defending their choices on potential life circumstances, they gained academic strength and solid critical thinking skills.

The years went by and I became a classroom teacher myself, and then went on and got a Master's degree in K-12 education, and then a Ph.D. in education. For my doctorate, I studied learning acquisition and spent considerable time on social and emotional learning techniques.

As a teacher, I tried out Conundrums in the inner city classroom and it worked very well – my class loved answering the questions and engaged in vigorous and intellectually stimulating class discussions. I discovered that this methodology worked exceptionally well with kids coming from a disadvantaged environment. I believe that using Conundrums in the classroom helped my students learn critical problem-solving skills that they may not have been exposed to at home.

My own children got older and one day not too long ago we were sitting around reminiscing about "the good old days" when we played Conundrums almost every time we got into the car. Kristen and Ian, now adults, suggested that we write down some of our favorites we had developed over the years so that we could share them with others.

Parents and grandparents, teachers and substitutes, babysitters and any other adult who would like to increase the critical thinking skills of children may use Conundrum to assist in that endeavor. Conundrum is designed to increase social and emotional skills, provide common (and sometimes not-so-common) scenarios for a child to work through, and to let a child's imagination soar. Along with imaginative play comes sequencing skills (what would you do first...second...third?) and solid critical thinking skills with ethics and morals at the center. The best part about the game is that it is FUN. Kids love to be challenged and they love to create and defend choices. Conundrum increases verbal skills and helps children formulate and express their ideas, all while exploring exciting and interesting topics.

This book is easy to use. A few tips are found on the next pages, and then the Conundrums begin.

Note: Please read the Teaching with Conundrums section before beginning to play the game. At the end of the book are indexes by category so if a child or class is particularly interested in a particular area, parents, grandparents, or teachers may begin with those before branching out into other areas.

We hope you enjoy using this book as a tool and a fun learning opportunity for both you and the children you love.

Sincerely,

Alisa Griffis, Ph.D.
Ian Xander
Kristen Xander Flores

How and When to Play Conundrum

This book contains conundrums that range from easiest to hardest. You know your children best – so you can select (and modify!) any conundrum to fit your own child's needs and emotional level.

The easiest conundrums are generally designed for Pre-k to 2nd grade children. These are simple choices for developing critical thinkers.

The mid-level conundrums are generally for 1st through 4th grade children. Some of the conundrums are still quite simple, but others begin to range upward in complexity. This is for children who are becoming more skilled at analysis and critical thinking skills.

The final level is for 4th through 7th graders. These conundrums are much more complex and are designed for students who are reaching higher levels of emotional maturity and cognitive thinking skills. There are a variety of themes in this level that may not be appropriate for every child, so adult discretion in selection is suggested.

Help is given for parents for the first 140 or so Conundrums, with some suggestions of likely answers and some potential considerations for answers. If you've got any questions about appropriate answers, ask us on our FaceBook page ("Conundrum Kids") and we'll answer you quickly!

Anyone Can Play

Kids have all sorts of interests, ability levels, observational skills, and so forth. If you have a child who is older, but has never been exposed to critical thinking of this nature, you may wish to start in the lower categories and then range upward as his or her skills begin to increase. Adults like to answer conundrum questions, too.

How Many Can Play?

Conundrum is ideal for 2 – 6 players, although it can be modified for classroom use or for individual children.

Rules to Conundrum

For 2 – 6 players.

1) **Begin:** Ask the question and give the kids two or more minutes to think about their responses. No one is allowed to jump in or shout, "I know! I know!" during that quiet thinking time.

   (This develops "wait time" and teaches kids the value of thinking before they speak.)

2) **Answering:** Kids take turns answering the question. Any methodology works for this: Picking a number, drawing a name out of a hat, volunteer, going clockwise, going by age (and switching it around, of course), and so forth.

3) **Listening:** The others must listen without groaning or making other derogatory sounds when someone is talking. No "active" listening (asking questions) – quite literally, everyone simply *listens*.

4) **Rebuttal:** After everyone has gone, there can be an optional rebuttal time where kids get to refute the contentions made by the other(s) with logical thinking. This rebuttal time is excellent for kids in the 4th grade and above.

5) **Defense:** If you include a rebuttal time, you should also have a "defense" time (just like in a court of law) where the child who was rebutted can either "see the light" (change) or "stand by the idea". They must defend whichever option they select.

6) **Finishing:** The round is over when everyone has had a chance. The adult(s) present can then share their point of view – but carefully. This is all about developing a child's ability to think something through – not to be a parent's parrot or to be controlled or manhandled into thinking a particular way. By giving a reasoned (with evidence/resources) response to the children and then to end with, "You can think about that" is plenty.

Note: It is best for children to answer no more than four or five "Conundrums" at any one time, and it is fine for them to answer just one (they'll generally beg for more, but it is fine to say, "Let's do some later!").

For One Child:

The parent can play the devil's advocate or ask additional questions to deepen the child's thinking.

For Classroom Use:

For groups larger than six students, not everyone will have a chance to answer each question. Instead, the teacher or substitute or group leader may call on children using a random method (such as drawing a popsicle stick with the children's names on it out of a jar or calling from the roll sheet) or by asking for volunteers.

If asking for volunteers, be aware of the shy or quiet child who is hesitant to answer, but who may need this activity to develop critical thinking skills. Don't force a child to answer ("pass" is perfectly acceptable), but do kindly encourage it. If the ground rules are enforced so that there is never any mocking or blurting out from other students – most children will eventually feel safe sharing their ideas/opinions.

It is also possible to form "Conundrum Circles" within the classroom. Students may be divided up into small groups of 4-6, and then a leader in the group (the position can rotate with each conundrum asked) chooses a conundrum and the game begins.

If choosing to create Conundrum Circles in the classroom, it is best to play and model the game whole-class for several sessions so that students understand the game and how it is played. This will keep the focus upon the conundrums and the answers, and not upon the process of the game itself.

Have fun!

When to Use Conundrums:

- When driving in the car
- On a rainy day
- After school
- After homework
- At a grandparent's house
- At a birthday party
- As a "sponge" (fill-in) activity at school
- With a babysitter
- When you've got some spare time – grab the book and begin!

Benefits to Conundrums:

Prepare children for common life challenges

Create more thoughtful individuals

Expand imagination

Promote & develop critical thinking skills

Become skilled at considering many different variables

Prepare children for difficult life situations

Increase the ability to think ethically

Augment listening ability

Develop simple debate and rebuttal techniques

Learn how to respond appropriately

Advance verbal skills

Sequence choices in an orderly fashion

Be trained not to make snap judgments

Discover there are many points-of-view

Realize that different people have different tastes

Become comfortable with thinking outside the box

Get to know siblings, classmates, and others' interests

Open up the world of possibilities

Bond with parents and/or teachers

Teaching with Conundrums

It is perfectly appropriate and acceptable to jot down a few notes under the various Conundrum questions. Most adults find that the time to do this is after the child has answered the questions and when the child is not looking/aware that notes have been made.

The purpose of recording some data is multifold.

1) To assist you in remembering what needs to be revisited in a week or two.

This happens when a child answers something in a way that reflects some moral or ethical concerns or safety concerns.

Parents and adults should not attempt to correct a child during the Conundrum answer period. Instead, note the answer the child made, and then later on (3 days to two weeks later), during a calm time (when the child and parent are well-rested and in a peaceful mood), use the "Story Telling" or "Modeling" method to engage the child.

Do not ask the child to recall his or her answer ("When you said _____ during the Conundrum from last week that was wrong!"). Children will be able to make a connection independently. Conundrum Kids is always supposed to be a positive and uplifting way of learning.

2) To document progress forward when revisiting a Conundrum.

(Many children enjoy being asked the same Conundrum again and again over time).

3) To note the answers that were acceptable, so you will not need to revisit that question in the future unless a child asks for that Conundrum again. If a child answers immediately in the way that he or she should, then the parent can check off the Conundrum.

It is possible to have several children answering and have one or two be accurate/appropriate in their answers and have other children not be developmentally, socially, intellectually, or emotionally on target yet.

4) If you're going through Conundrums with a child, and the child is off-base on virtually every answer, this becomes a wonderful tool to work with your child daily and help him or her grow.

In the beginning, some children are quite naive or unrealistic in their responses. This is pretty typical. As children "play" the game of Conundrum, they begin to develop stronger communication skills and cognitive abilities.

Sometimes parents may feel that their child is not growing rapidly and gaining skills quickly enough. Children develop at different rates. A child who is unable to answer many Conundrums well may need to back up a bit and answer some of the simpler Conundrums first. Refer to the Index under "Beginner Conundrums." If a child still struggles, Conundrum Kids: Tiny Tots might be an excellent starting place. The Tiny Tots book focuses on developing basic choice-making skills and "precursor" skills necessary for a child to be successful with older-kid Conundrums.

The Story-Telling Method of Teaching Children

The story-telling method of teaching is when a parent creates a make-believe story that is either realistic or clearly fantasy-based and uses the story to teach a lesson to the children.

Stories like Pinocchio began as a way for children to learn that lying has consequences. This is an example of a fantasy-based story designed to teach a lesson. Stories do not have to be as long and detailed as a full-length feature film! They can be very short.

An example of a realistic story is to use the "When I was a kid" or "When Grandma was a kid" or "I once knew a kid…" method where the parent then tells a story about "someone else" and the trouble they got into and the consequences from that trouble.

Parents can also locate already written picture books, read-aloud books, movies, and short films and use those to help supplement their teaching.

Interestingly, the parent does not have to explicitly point out that the story or movie that they are introducing is designed to teach a child some important skill. It's better to actively watch the movie/read the story with the child, but not turn it into a preachy moment. Children learn best when they think THEY are drawing their own conclusions. A canny parent can ask questions like, "I was sad when ____ happened. What were you feeling?" or "Why do you think the kid did that?" and then listen to the child learning from the experience.

The Modeling Method of Teaching Children

In this method, parents act out a specific and pre-planned scenario. The parent talks out loud and lets the child hear his or her thought process while solving the problem.

This is the "Oh, look!" type of scenario that goes like this:

"Oh, look! I just found a ring on the ground! It's really pretty. The person who has lost it is going to feel so sad! I will give the ring to the store manager so that when the owner returns, she will be able to have her ring back." Then, after turning the ring over to the store manager, the parent/adult can say, "I feel so much better knowing that I did the right thing by turning the ring in."

The child has just learned through example. A parent should do no more than this.   There is no need to revisit this or talk about it any longer at that time. The modeling out-loud approach IS the teaching methodology.

The way to discover if a child has learned is to ask a similar Conundrum question in a few weeks.

The sneaky key is to never be obvious in one's teaching. Children (and adults) do not like being lectured, so by using the story-telling and modeling methods of teaching, children will learn important life lessons in a way that is enjoyable.

Conundrums

Conundrum #1:

It's raining outside. What are you going to wear to school?

Secondary question: How will you protect your books and homework?

Kids should be thinking along the lines of:

- Warm jacket
- Umbrella
- Boots or shoes that won't absorb water

- Hold book/backpack in front under umbrella
- Plastic bag around books
- Keep backpack on back but under umbrella

Notes:

Conundrum #2:

Your best friend took your favorite book and hasn't given it back yet. List three things that you could do to get it back, and then pick the best of those three things and explain why it's the best choice.

Kids might list:

- Ask the friend nicely (in person)
- Tell the friend's parents

- Have your mom (or dad) ask the friend
- Have your mom or dad ask the friend's parents
- Shout at your friend
- Send your friend a note at school
- E-mail your friend
- Phone your friend
- Stop by their house to pick it up (with or without a parent present)

Notes:

Conundrum #3:

Your parents give you money for lunch, but a friend is offering to sell you a toy. Do you spend it on the toy, or do you buy food with it? Explain your choice.

> *Secondary Questions:*
> If you picked the food option, but you still want the toy, what could you do to earn it?
>
> If you picked the toy option, what are you going to tell your parents, and what will you do about eating lunch?

Kids should be thinking along the lines of:
- Buy lunch

BUT – they can do chores to buy the toy if they want it, or trade with the friend for something else.

If kids pick the toy option, they should tell their parents, and for lunch, they won't eat. If they say they will bum food off of other people, it leads to an open discussion later on about how people should stand on their own two feet and not ask others for help when they already have the resources available to them.

Notes:

Conundrum #4:

You want to have a pet, but your parents say you aren't responsible enough. What would you do to earn their trust?

List five things that you could do – then pick the top two and defend your choice…why are those two the best to pick out of the five? Why?

Consider: For younger kids, have them list 3 things they could do and pick their top choice.

Notes:

Conundrum #5:

You have some homework due, but your friends want you to play at their house. What can you do to work this out so you can do both? Or – do you have to pick just one thing or the other?

Kids should be thinking along the lines of:

Do the homework first, play later.
If it's a lot of homework, split it up. Do an hours'
worth, play for 2 or 3 hours, and then finish the
homework (if this is a weekend). If it's on a weekday
– do the homework first, and schedule a play date on
another day.

Notes:

Conundrum #6:

You don't study for your spelling test and your friend
offers to let you cheat off of his paper. Do you take
up his offer or do you possibly fail the test? Explain
your thinking.

Kids should be thinking along the lines of:

- Fail the test and study better next time.

If the child says he or she is going to cheat, this will
lead to questions later in the week along the lines of:
Why is cheating wrong? What are the consequences
of cheating?

Notes:

Conundrum #7:

Your mom lets you pick what you're going to eat for dinner. Everyone in the family will have to eat the same thing. What will you pick, and why? Defend your choice.

Hint: Ideally, kids should pick items that everyone would enjoy. This teaches them to be considerate of others, instead of selfishly only selecting what they, themselves like (but maybe someone else cannot eat because of an allergy or other need).

Notes:

Conundrum #8:

You break a friend's bike – the chain on it is broken in half because you rode it into a tree. He isn't there at the time. What are you going to do? What will you do next? How will you tell your parents…or will you?

Kids should be thinking along the lines of:

Wheel the bike home (or call someone to pick you up)
Ask a parent to help fix it
Save the money for the chain repair
Tell the friend and apologize
Have your parents call the friend's parents and talk it out

Notes:

Conundrum #9:

You're playing basketball at lunch and another kid wants to play that everyone else doesn't like. Do you let her play, or do you turn her away? Explain your answer.

Kids should be thinking along the lines of:

Let the kid play (this is the best answer)
OR
Do something else with the kid at the next recess or after school

Notes:

Conundrum #10:

You decide not to let someone play tag with you because no one likes him or her. Later on, you feel guilty. What could you do to solve the problem you created?

Kids should be thinking along the lines of:

Apologize to the kid and include him or her the next time.

Notes:

Conundrum #11:

You drop your spelling book in a water puddle. You pick it up quickly and shake it off, and try to dry it as best as you can – but half of it is ruined. What are you going to do???

Kids should be thinking along the lines of:

- Explain to the teacher what happened and share with a friend.
- Blow it dry with a blow dryer.
- Let it dry naturally, it might be better than one thinks after it's dried
- Get copies made out of a clean, undamaged book and use those

Notes:

Conundrum #12:

There are three bullies on the playground. They sometimes pick on you and your friends. Name three things that you can do to stop them.

Two have to be non-violent. Defend which would be the best of the three choices and why.

Consider: Kids will often pick the "I'll hit them" choice. This is normal. But if we just say, "NO" – it doesn't help them to think it through. Instead, you want to listen carefully and ask them to think through their choices and defend the best one. If they come up with something truly lousy, the very best choice to ask is, "Why won't that work?"

Notes:

Conundrum #13:

You want to watch TV but you have schoolwork to do. Your mom says you have to do your schoolwork first, but you're going to miss your show. You can't record the show. What are you going to do?

Notes:

Conundrum #14:

You break your dad's favorite coffee cup. Little bits of the handle & the rest of the mug scatter everywhere – even under the refrigerator. You have bare feet – and so do your brothers and sisters. What are you going to do? Come up with a plan and put it in order of first, second, third and so on.

Kids should be thinking along the lines of:

Tell everyone to stand still.

The person farthest from the glass should put on shoes and bring shoes for the others.
Start the sweep-up process. Use a broom and dustpan.
Tell your dad what happened.

Notes:

Conundrum #15:

You are standing with your mom in front of an ATM machine. The lady in front of you walks away and drops $100 out of her purse. What are you going to do?

Consider: When kids say that they will keep the money, this is a natural inclination even though we adults know that the right thing to do is return it. If a child says they'd keep the money, ask, "Why is that hurting someone else?"

Notes:

Conundrum #16:

Your mom makes you wear really geeky clothes. Do you tell her to stop? Do you tell her what you want to wear, or do you just wear them to keep her happy?

Secondary question: If you wear them just to keep her happy, how do you keep from getting teased at school?

If you ask her to let you wear other clothes, how do you ask so that you don't hurt her feelings?

Notes:

Conundrum #17:

You have a teacher in school that you don't like. She sits at her desk and shouts at you and the other students. You don't "get" a math problem, but you know if you raise your hand, she's going to shout. You're not allowed to ask anyone else in the class for help or she's going to shout.

What do you do?

Kids should be thinking along the lines of:

Ask help from a student at recess or lunch.
Ask for tutoring after school (or before school) from someone else.
Tell your parent or other adult how the teacher responds.

Notes:

Conundrum #18:

Your best friend is moving in three months. You've been friends since you were little. What are you going to do in the last three months? Name some things that you can do to make good memories.

Secondary Question: After he or she moves – will you keep in touch? How???

Kids should be thinking along the lines of:

Hang out with them a lot
Help them pack
Make a video of you two doing things together (and/or put together a multimedia montage of photos and film clips)
Go to the movies or go bike riding together
Take photographs and make an album for you both
Make a memory album with photos, drawings, and captions

To keep in touch: E-mail, telephone, social media (if this is allowed in the family), visits if possible.

Notes:

Conundrum #19:

You've been sneaking your dog in to sleep with you night after night. How do you make sure that your mom doesn't find out??? Defend your logic.

Parents: This is not a question that encourages complete honesty…but when asked this question, kids may come to the better conclusion that they need to talk it over and tell their parents. They also might need to have a discussion with the parents on why they would like to sleep with their pet.

Notes:

Conundrum #20:

Your mom finds out your dog has been sleeping with you even though she has forbidden it. How do you calm her down? What should your punishment be? How can you explain to your mom why you want the dog to sleep with you?

How do you calm her down?

Some potential choices:
Apologize right away
Face up and admit it (don't keep lying)
Speak calmly
Don't get mad and shout back

Reasons why a child might want the dog to sleep with him or her:

Protection
Feel loved
It's fun
They are warm

Consider: The real question here is why is the parent <u>not </u>allowing the dog in the room/bed? Are the parents being too strict? Is the dog making the child feel safe and/or loved?

Sometimes children do sneaky things because they feel a sense of unrighteousness/injustice over a rule that makes no sense to them. Maybe the parents just don't want to deal with dog hair/shedding. Maybe the dog can have a bed by the side of the child's bed, or put a special blanket on the bed that the dog can sleep upon. Maybe the child will have to be responsible with cleaning the bedding.

This could be an opportunity to teach your child about compromise.

Notes:

Conundrum #21:

Name three ways to get someone to stop yelling at you.

Kids should be thinking along the lines of:

Don't yell back
Tell a joke
Nod head and listen without making faces
Answer quietly/softly
Be reasonable
Avoid frustration
Apologize if you've done something wrong

Conundrum #22:

Your mom tells you to scrub the toilet for the first time on your own. She's busy and can't help you. You get dishwashing liquid and put it into the toilet. What is going to happen? If that DOES happen – what are you going to do about it?

Kids should be thinking along the lines of:

The toilet is likely to get filled with tons of bubbles
The kid should scoop out the bubbles and put them in the bathtub, shower, or sink
Look up how to clean a toilet on the Internet

Notes:

Conundrum #23:

You have a really awful haircut and your mom wants you to keep on wearing your hair that way. You respect your mom, so what are some ways that you can solve this problem peacefully without just stubbornly telling her, "no."

Kids should be thinking along the lines of:

Find pictures of good haircuts that you like and show them to your mom.
Explain calmly why you'd like your hair a particular way
Talk about your feelings.

Notes:

Conundrum #24:

There's a book you really, really, really want to read, but your parents won't let you. Tell some reasons why you think parents would forbid certain books?

Kids should be thinking along the lines of:

- There is adult content that a kid should not know about
- It's far above your reading level
- There might be things that are immoral that are in the book.
- Maybe it's too violent
- Maybe it's too sad and they don't want me to be sad
- Maybe they are afraid that I will start doing some of the things in the book.
- Maybe there will be destructive or dangerous things in the book.
- Maybe for religious reasons.

Notes:

Conundrum #25:

Is there ever a time and a place to try to convince parents that they are wrong?

Secondary Question: If you say that there is – what respectful things can you do?

If you say that there isn't – how can you get over being disappointed?

Kids should be thinking along the lines of:

Yes, there is a time and a place, BUT they need to be respectful and have a calm discussion.

If a child says that there is never a time and a place to convince parents that they are wrong:

Kids can get over their disappointment by doing something physical, fun, or productive that they CAN do.

Notes:

Conundrum #26:

Your parents don't like you reading after bedtime. Do you slip a flashlight under the covers and continue reading anyways?

Secondary Question: What are some of the consequences that could happen to you for reading late into the night?

Potential consequences:

Tired or can't get up in the morning
Grouchy in the morning
Get in trouble and get book and/or flashlight taken away

Parents: This is a tricky conundrum because even though we want our kids to go to sleep and be well rested, we WANT them to be voracious readers that just cannot put down a book. One of the purposes of this question is to get kids to realize that they SHOULD want to keep reading!!! It was not written to actually get kids to say that they should not do this – but to subtly implant the suggestion that reading late IS cool! One "compromise" that a parent could offer is "Read late on Friday and Saturday nights" or "Let's start reading earlier so you can read longer," etc.

This can then lead to a discussion on how fun reading is, etc.

Notes:

Conundrum #27:

You hate peas. You've scooped them into your lap at dinner to hide them. What is going to happen if your parents find out? Name at least three things that they might do. Which one would they do first?

Kids should be thinking along the lines of:

Get shouted at
Have the peas scooped up and mashed in your face (hopefully parents wouldn't really do that!)
Restriction
Have to do the dishes
Make you eat them anyways
Give you more peas to eat
Laugh (it could happen!)

Make you do chores or other things
Check your lap every evening

Note: You might be asking yourself, "What is it about the peas?" If a child hates a food, there are many ways to get them to eat them. One thing that we did in our family was to say, "You're ___ years old, so you have to eat ___ peas" (as in: You're 7 years old, so you have to eat 7 peas). Another thing we did was to say to the child, "I know you don't like peas and we're having them tonight. You will need to eat some. Would you rather have 1 tablespoon, or 2 tablespoons?" (and after that: "Would you rather measure them out or would you like me to measure it for you?").

One of the things that children do is get into food battles because it is their opportunity to control their world. If a child has MANY food dislikes, this might be a sign that they need to be offered many choices in other areas their lives: "Would you like this toothpaste or that toothpaste?" "Would you like to me to buy you the red shirt or the blue shirt?" "Would you like to get up at 8:00 or 9:00?" (on a Saturday). "Would you like to read this book or that book?" Etc. By giving children many choices all day long, they start to feel respected and in control. This reduces their need to control their eating.

If a child generally likes many different foods and is not controlling his or her eating through food – then it is okay for a child to dislike a food or two. If that is the case, consider not serving them that food. Those battles are not worth having if the child is generally amiable and eats a wide variety of foods.

If a child does not eat a wide variety of foods, then a parent may need to start to expand the eating horizons without it becoming a big battle. Serving a food in tiny portions is often helpful. "Hiding it" in other types of food that the child likes can help (making a stew that the child likes, for example, and putting in a small amount of carrots). Another way to help expand foods eaten is to have the child cook with you. When he/she is able to chop and cook the foods, they often are more willing to eat them. Another way is to put butter or sugar on the food (within reason, and clearly on things that taste good with butter or sugar) and then after the child is used to it that way and likes it – wean the butter or sugar out of it. They'll never know that it's not there if each time the amount of butter or turkey/beef bacon or sugar (or whatever "crutch" is used) is cut down by ¼. Within 4 servings…no more crutch. I never told my kids if I was doing this last methodology – I just made the food taste very appealing to begin with and then weaned them off of the secondary taste.

Notes:

Conundrum #28:

You told one of your friends that you would hang out with them on Friday night. A new friend wants you to do something totally cool the same night. Who do you choose, and why?

Kids should be thinking along the lines of: They already made a commitment to the first friend.

Notes:

Conundrum #29:

You're having a birthday party and you have to invite two of your friends. They DO NOT get along with each other. You plan to invite both – but what are you going to do to keep them from getting into a fight? Name three things that you can do to keep your party fun.

Kids should be thinking along the lines of:

- Plan some team games and put them on different teams.
- Don't seat them near each other.
- Make sure a parent knows so that they can run interference as necessary.
- Talk to each one privately beforehand and explain they are your friend and that's why you invited them, but that other person is also a friend, and ask them to either get along or ignore each other.
- Recognize that one friend may chose not to come – and that is their own decision, and does not reflect upon you, but upon them.
- Spend your time equally with your friends at the party (do not favor one or another).

Consider: This conundrum was worded carefully so that the child would learn that he/she could ask two "warring" friends to a party. So many children think that they have to "pick one and exclude one" but that's not always the best choice for a lot of reasons. By having children work through proactive methodologies, this helps them hone their social skills and it helps them think about how to handle an upcoming social situation BEFORE the situation blows up.

Notes:

Conundrum #30:

Your brother wants you to help with chores, but you have other plans. Plus – you really hate helping out with chores. What are you going to do? What do you say? How do you handle this?

Kids should be thinking along the lines of:

Offer a trade-off.

Notes:

Conundrum #31:

From the list of chores below, pick which one would be your favorite, and why? Defend your choice.

- Taking care of the pets: (Cleaning up the doggie doo-doo, giving them food and water, and/or cleaning the kitty litter box)

- Doing outside yard work: (Sweeping up in front of the house, trimming plants, bagging up weeds & trash)

- Cleaning inside the house: (Dusting and vacuuming & emptying trash cans)

Notes:

Conundrum #32:

If you can be any wild animal, which one would you be, and why?

Note: This is a good conundrum for younger children for several reasons.

First, the parent can then determine if the child knows what a wild animal IS. If a child starts listing dogs and cats and so forth…then the parent can ask them, "What makes an animal wild?"

Second, the "why" portion of the answer is good for any age child, for this can give you a clue to the child's core personality, or what some of their needs are. Maybe they need to feel powerful or protected or maybe they need to feel loved or cuddled or sweet or cute…there are many clues that can be found in these answers.

In some cases, children might pick something that is disturbing to the parent (an alligator so that I can eat people). This might not be a sign of anything pathological or alarming. If a series of disquieting answers are given over time, a parent may wish to seek the help and guidance from a professional. One or two instances of "the shocking answer" for any of the conundrums may just be a child who is mischievous or rascally and/or looking for a reaction because they know that they can exasperate their parents. One of the ways to tell the difference between a child who is looking to provoke a response and one that may need professional assessment would be to look at the child's general reactions to everyday events. If a child is generally good-natured, balanced, and personable and gets along well with others – then an unusual or surprising answer or two to a conundrum should not be any cause for alarm.

If a child has a pattern of being mercurial (rapidly changeable), disagreeable, and having tantrums, then the answers to the conundrums should be recorded (written down when not in the presence of the child) and used as examples when speaking to a physician or a therapist.

Notes:

Conundrum #33:

If you could be any house pet, which one would you be and why? Here are some possibilities to spark your imagination.

Cat	Snake
Dog	Rat
Bird (like: Parakeet,	Mouse
Parrot, Cockatiel)	Lizard
Hamster	Fish

Consider: There are many other animals that a child can select. If a child selects a tiger or other clearly and obviously wild animal, one can say, "Oh, that's a great choice…but that is a wild animal! For this conundrum, I'd like you to pick an animal that can live safely inside a home with humans and be a pet."

Notes:

Conundrum #34:

If you could live in one of these places, which would you pick, and why?

- Big city sky rise apartment
- Suburban tract home
- Small community
- Farm
- Country (with not many people living near you)
- Forest

Consider: The "why" answer is the most important portion of this conundrum. You are learning about your child's dispositions and likes and dislikes. It also helps you determine if a child knows what some of these words mean. If a child is younger – describe what "suburban tract home" means, and what "small community" means, etc. Conundrums like this help increase vocabulary as well as help increase a child's ability to articulate their interests.

Many children will select the exact same environment in which they live. If they do this, ask them a different question later: If you could pick some other place to live, what would it be?

Notes:

Conundrum #35:

The power goes out and your parents aren't home. What do you do?

Kids should be thinking along the lines of:

Get flashlights
(the problem with lighting a candle is that it could start a fire – this could be a great discussion with younger children. An older child might be able to light a thick candle on a plate or saucer in the middle of a table without causing a problem).

Other choices might include:
Put on extra clothes if the heater also goes off and it's cold.
Keep the door locked.
Use the phone to contact the parents if the phones are working.
Stay calm.
Read a book by flashlight.

Notes:

Conundrum #36:

Your neighbor has lost a cat. Where are you going to help look for the cat? How long will you help them? What sorts of things do you say to the neighbor to encourage him or her?

Kids should be thinking along the lines of:

Up in trees
Under bushes
Help until it starts to get dark
Tell the neighbor that it'll be okay – you're sure the cat will come home and be just fine.

Consider: This is a way that a child predator could use to entice a child into a home, car, or other way to take a child. Without frightening a youth – one needs to make sure the child knows that the FIRST thing they should do is inform their parent immediately before looking for any animal or lost item with a neighbor, family friend, or stranger. Depending upon your child's age, fear-levels, and maturity, you may wish to explain that sometimes there are people who haven't really lost their pet (or item) and that they really are trying to get familiar with a child for 'bad' purposes.

Notes:

Conundrum #37:

Your parents have told you not to have anyone over when they are not home. But your friend next door is at home alone and is scared. What are you going to do?

Kids should be thinking along the lines of:

You should call your parents first to let them know.
You should ask the friend why they are scared.
If your friend is your age and you know them well, and if it is safe, they should come over.

Parents: Kids might suggest that they go over to the friend's house, but that is not a great suggestion for many reasons. If it is safe, the friend should come over to YOUR house. If it is not safe and you are not nearby, then the parents (you) should call another trusted adult nearby and have them go straight over.

Notes:

Conundrum #38:

You are home alone and your parents told you you're not allowed to use the computer or watch TV. What three other things could you do to stay busy and out of trouble?

Kids should be thinking along the lines of:

Read books
Play a game

Do homework
Do a craft
Write a card or letter
Color/draw
Play in the back yard (if allowed to go outside)

Consider: What to say/do if a child lists something potentially dangerous or destructive to do when alone: Say, "You said _____. Why might that not be a good idea?"

Notes:

Conundrum #39:

If you could be invisible and you were allowed to go anywhere and see anything – what would you do?

Note: This type of question enables you to understand the workings of your child's mind. If he or she chooses something heroic (even if it's impossible in real life), or if he or she chooses something innocuous that is in no way harmful or illegal, just listen and enjoy.

If the child chooses something that is clearly immoral or unethical (sneak into a theatre to see a movie, steal something, etc), you can then bring up the discussion on integrity being "always doing the right thing when no one is looking."

This sort of teaching can then be followed up several times over the next couple of months by pointing out a few other situations where someone with integrity would do the right thing, even if no one else were looking.

One of the keys to training a child in both critical thinking skills and in moral aptitude/choices is to use the "teach and revisit" method. By revisiting a core concept at least two additional times scattered across a one-month period of time, it begins to solidify the concept in the child's mind.

After that, "talk out loud" becomes another excellent teaching tool. The parent can then select simple topics that they are "struggling" with and "talk it out loud" with the child. For example, a parent can say something like, "The lady at the store gave me $1.00 too much in change. I knew that no one would ever find out if I kept the dollar, but I wouldn't feel right about that. The right thing to do is to return the money. I do not steal. So…I gave it back to her. That is integrity. Doing the right thing even though no one else would ever find out."

It is tricky to listen to children come up with something that is clearly immoral or unethical. If a parent reacts and says, "That's wrong!" the child will only have a feeling (negative/shame), but may not learn the actual lesson. The key to conundrums is to have the child explain and give their reasoning, and then to ask, "Why isn't that the best choice?" This helps the child to re-align the thinking process and come up with other viable alternatives.

Notes:

Conundrum #40:

If you have just ONE superpower – what would you pick and what would you do with it?

Consider: This gives you the opportunity to discover some more of your child's character and dispositions. Often the superpower chosen relates to a child's needs or insecurities in life. Then at a different time, a parent (not even mentioning the super power) can talk with the child about whatever was revealed.

Kids just LOVE answering these questions – and sometimes their answers have no "deeper" meaning! Sometimes it's just "this is FUN." It enables their minds to explore and their imaginations to develop. What fun!

Notes:

Conundrum #41:

Who is your favorite superhero? Why?

Consider: This is similar to Conundrum #40 – and the child's responses enable them to articulate their reasons why a particular superhero is heroic. If a child picks an anti-hero (a dastardly villain), then just rephrase the question and explain that they have to pick a hero, not a villain).

Notes:

Conundrum #42

If you were given $1,000 what would you do with it?

Note: Although we always want to "teach, teach, teach" – this conundrum isn't really the place for that unless a child picks something shocking and surprising like, "buy a gun." Generally kids will pick innocuous things like buy clothes, candy, go to Disneyland, buy books, games, toys, etc.

This is not the time to start saying things like, "But you must tithe 10% to God" or "What about helping out a poor relation?" because these other items can be learned in other ways and via other conundrums. It is okay to just let a child's imagination soar.

Even if the item that the child wants to pick doesn't match up to the $1,000 – for younger children, it's best to ignore it. For older children (8 and up), then one can say, "Oh, me too! I'd love a Mercedes! Sadly, they cost $50,000 and we've only got $1,000 to spend. How would you spend $1,000?"

Notes:

Conundrum #43:

What is the best hair color? Explain your answer, then defend your thinking.

Notes:

Conundrum #44:

Your friend calls you at 6:00 at night, crying because she hasn't started her project that's due tomorrow. You're already finished with yours. Would you help her? How much help might you give?

Kids should be thinking along the lines of:

- Give a few suggestions
- Ask a few questions
- If he/she is close by and it's okay – you might be able to go over for an hour to help.

What kids should NOT do: Do the project for the friend (either at your house or their house).

Notes:

Conundrum #45:

You want to go to the movies with your friend but he or she doesn't have any money. You only have enough for yourself. What do you do instead?

Variation: What do you do to earn the money to take him or her?

Kids should be thinking along the lines of:

Do some other activity with the friend.

Go to the movies with someone else either that day or another day

Earn money by doing chores and treat the friend

Notes:

Conundrum #46:

What is your favorite kind of weather, and why?

Notes:

Conundrum #47:

You are alone on a boat on a lake. It springs a leak. What are you going to do?

Kids should be thinking along the lines of:

- Immediately begin towards shore.
- Be sure the life jacket is on securely.
- Bail out the boat as you go along.
- Stick something into the hole to stop the leak.
- Phone an adult with a cell phone while doing the other items as well.

Notes:

Conundrum #48:

The washing machine was going and you threw in your favorite red shirt and it turned the entire white wash bright pink. What do you do?

Kids should be thinking along the lines of:

Ask a parent how to bleach clothes.
Look up the answer on the Internet.
Bleach the clothes that are pink BEFORE they go into the dryer!
Don't dry the clothes – wash them again with bleach.
Wear pink underwear for a very long time.

Notes:

Conundrum #49:

You are playing a game with your siblings and ended up breaking your mom's favorite vase. How do you solve the problem?

Kids should be thinking along the lines of:

- Clean it up and save the pieces if possible.
- Wear gloves/shoes while cleaning it up
- Tell the parent.
- Buy the parent another vase with savings or earnings.

Notes:

Conundrum #50:

You don't know how to multiply as well as your classmates – what do you do to solve the problem?

Kids should be thinking along the lines of:
- Make flashcards and practice at home.
- Do timed drills.
- Practice only the ones that you do not know.
- Spend 10 minutes every day practicing.
- Drill with a friend/sibling/parent.

Notes:

Conundrum #51:

Your friend has asked you to baby sit his pet hamster for the weekend. Your parents would never approve, so you hide it in your closet. What are you going to do to take care of the hamster? What could go wrong? What would happen if your parents found out?

Kids should be thinking along the lines of:

- Give it fresh water and food.
- It could escape.
- It could get killed by the cat or the dog.
- If the parents found out, the child would be on restriction or in trouble/on punishment in some way.

Consider: This opens the door to a conversation about being sneaky and how it is not the right thing to do. Kids often don't know how a parent will REALLY react to having a weekend pet-visitor (or other event). Kids sometimes think that a parent will object when they really will not.

This can lead to an open discussion with a child (or children) about not assuming that a parent is going to say, "no."

There are several other issues in this conundrum: Doing something dishonest is not right. Even if the parents really would say "no" – it might be for extremely good reasons (someone has an allergy, there is no safe place for the pet because of other pets, there are going to be visitors whose small children could harm the pet, the family is going out of town themselves that weekend).

Children also assume that they are the ONLY person who could watch a pet, but pet owners generally have many different options and people to ask. Kids sometimes don't think of that option – they only think that they'd love to do something and that no one else could ever do that particular task/chore/obligation.

It also brings up the question, "Why would a child assume that you would say no?" Only if there were truly compelling reasons (and "inconvenience" is not a compelling reason) should a child not be allowed to pet-sit a small animal for a few days. Pet sitting develops maturity and many other skills.

Notes:

Conundrum #52:

If you decided to live in a tree, what would you take with you and how would you live there?

Kids should be thinking along the lines of:

- Something to sleep on (build some sort of platform)
- Something to sleep in (warmth)
- Food
- Some way to use the restroom
- A cell phone (how would it be charged?)
- Something to write on
- Something to read

Consider: My Side of the Mountain (independent reading level 6.7) is an excellent resource for living alone, as is Hatchet (independent reading level: grade 5.7) and Brian's Winter (independent reading level: 7.3). Another book fun "living alone" is From the Mixed up Files of Mrs. Basil E. Frankweiler (independent reading level 5.0). It's a dated book (no cell phones yet, etc), but it's very fun and imaginative reading.

These are really fun books for kids to read, or to hear during read-aloud times and can help open up discussions about why kids love the idea of living on their own and developing independent living skills. It does not encourage kids to run away to read these books.

That is not why children run away from home. They run away for truly pressing and urgent crises that are usually long-term and a long-time in development – and a wise parent knows to look for signs and to keep a living situation peaceful, fun, and filled with love and laughter.

Rule of Thumb: For read-aloud books, pick a book from 2 – 3 years above a child's independent reading level. Ask a teacher what your child's independent reading level is, or if you home school – conduct a test online by searching: free reading level assessment.

Notes:

Conundrum #53:

If you were trapped on a tropical island and you only had 5 things to take with you, what would you take so that you could live?

Kids should be thinking along the lines of:

- Sharp knife/pocket knife
- Rope/twine/cord
- Poncho/tarp
- Fireproof matches
- Saw
- Cooking pot/pan (dutch oven: best answer)
- Tent
- Pair of shoes
- Sharp axe
- Fishing pole & line

Parents: What if a child picks impractical items? This conundrum is VERY well played with a group of kids instead of just one, as the other children will begin to suggest practical things and as the kids go through the rebuttal phase, they can change their minds and revise to better solutions.

Notes:

Conundrum #54:

What is your favorite food and why?

Extension: What are the top 5 foods that you like, but none of them can have sugar in them?
Or: What are your favorite three veggies?

Notes:

Conundrum #55:

You drop a spoon in the garbage disposal and find out when you turn it on. What are you going to do?

Kids should be thinking along the lines of:

- Turn it off immediately.
- Leave it off and get it out (or get a parent)

62

Notes (for #55):

Conundrum #56:

Someone really close to you smells REALLY bad.
You really like him or her and don't want to embarrass
them. What do you do about it?

Kids should be thinking along the lines of:

- Talk to them privately.

That is really the best solution. The most mature
thing to do is to privately say to someone, "I really like
you and do not want to embarrass you, but I've
noticed that you've got some body odor. I wonder if
maybe it's your clothes that need washing?"

That way it takes the spotlight off the personal
hygiene of the individual and puts it onto the clothes.
It opens up a conversation. Most people know how to
then wash more frequently or figure out how to wash
out their clothing.

Notes:

Conundrum #57:

There's a bully at school and he's being mean to your friend. What do you do? You must support your decision with reasoning.

Kids should be thinking along the lines of:

- Tell a teacher
- Stand up to the bully
- Grab your friend and run
- Tell a parent
- Do nothing. It's not your problem (this is a potential answer, but you can ask your child/children, "Why is this not the best answer?"

Notes:

Conundrum #58:

Your parents are going out of town and you have to stay with the neighbors or a relative – but you don't like their kids. What do you do?

Kids should be thinking along the lines of:

- Bring activities that they can do independently/alone
- Bring something that maybe the other kids can do
- Suggest a friend's house instead

- Try compromising/being flexible with the other kids
- Figure out what it is they don't like about the kids and do different things

Notes:

Conundrum #59:

You have a magic pencil and it will write any story that you want it to write. What story will you write?

Consider: Kids can say anything they'd like. This is just creativity, but it does reveal a great deal about how a child's mind is working and what things are fun and adventuresome to them.

Notes:

Conundrum #60:

You have a magical eraser and it will erase anything you've done in the past. What will you erase?

Consider: Kids may be hesitant to actually say the real thing(s) that they've done. You can suggest that they'd think about it in their head, and then talk about it if they want to.

Notes:

Conundrum #61:

You have a set of colored pencils. Anything you draw comes to life. What will you draw?

Consider: This one leads to very interesting discussion, and can give parents insight into ways that they can assist their children in emotional or social growth and development. Also – one really fun question to ask after they've spoken, "What are some potential drawbacks to _____?" (Because if a kid draws a dinosaur and it comes to life…um….what if it's a T-Rex?).

Notes:

Conundrum #62:

What do you prefer more: Reading, Writing, Drawing, or playing with Play-Doh (or fill in some other toy)?

Consider: There are many Conundrums that are simply matters of personal preference, and there is no right or wrong answer. Asking, "Why?" is a great follow-up so that you can start to learn the child's preferences.

Variation: Have the child come up with something else he/she would rather do.

Notes:

Conundrum #63:

If you could have a magical pet, what would you have?

Some suggestion/ideas might be:

Dragon	Unicorn
Phoenix	Pegasus
Elf	Water horse (Loch
Fairy	Ness Monster)
Pixie	Leprechaun
Gnome	Mermaid

Notes:

Conundrum #64:

If you found a Genie and could ask for three wishes, but none of them could be for you (and you could not ask for more wishes), what would you ask for?

Consider: This is a great one for suggesting to kids that they think BIG, and also think of consequences! This is a very fun Conundrum that kids like revisit over and over again as they come up with new ideas on wishes.

This is a great time to work on their traits of empathy and charity. Encourage the children to think of other people and how they can help them (or animals).

Notes:

Conundrum #65:

You have to take care of the neighbor's dog while they are on vacation, but the dog is mean and scary. What do you do?

Kids should be thinking along the lines of:

- Bring an adult with you.
- Bring a toy/food for the dog
- Say, "No" and suggest that they need to find someone else
- Get to know the dog while the owners are there

Notes:

Conundrum #66:

If you were mean or rude to an adult and you felt sorry for it, how would you apologize?

Kids should be thinking along the lines of:

- Be very sincere
- Look them in the eyes
- Acknowledge that you were wrong
- Ask for forgiveness

Notes:

Conundrum #67:

What if you turned into Pinocchio and your nose grew every time you lied? What would you do?

Kids should be thinking along the lines of:

- Try to stop lying/not lie at all
- Get the nose fixed in some way
- Tell a family member what was happening

Notes:

Conundrum #68:

You're reaching for a book and the shelf that the book is on crashes to the ground. All of the books fall. What are you going to do?

Kids should be thinking along the lines of:

- Stack the books neatly
- Examine the shelf and try to figure out why it broke
- Try to fix it
- Replace the books
- Tell an adult or get help if any books are damaged or if the shelf cannot be fixed.

Notes:

Conundrum #69:

You are now the boss of the house. You have to make the rules in your house. What house rules would you install?

***Consider*:** This involves a great deal of creativity! This is a great time to see what your child places value in, and their emotional maturity. If they are going to say a bunch of "I...."

rules, such as, "I will no longer have any bedtime" and so forth show that the child is still self-centered and playful/wanting to break rules. This is not a bad thing! It's fun to find out what kids would really wish to do!

It's possible to have playful fun with your child and for a special day/holiday/birthday, they could get to do one of these new "rules" as a treat (For example – change the bedtime to 10:00 p.m.). This signals to children that their parents respect them – and it adds some spontaneity to day-to-day life.

Notes:

Conundrum #70:

You are going to be an adult for one day. What things would you do? What would you NOT want to do? What would be the hardest part? What would be the most fun part?

Consider: These questions should be asked one at a time – ask the first question and get answers. Then extend the Conundrum play time by asking the next question, etc.

There are no right or wrong answers – but adults may be quite surprised at how children view the role of adulthood.

Notes:

Conundrum #71:

You have $100, how would you spend it?

Consider: This conversation can lead to information about saving money and giving to charity. Many people consider 10% of an amount of money to be the appropriate amount to give to charity. It can also lead to a conversation about sales taxes or other costs (like having to buy batteries for a toy).

Notes:

Conundrum #72:

If you could go anywhere in the world, where would you go and how would you get there?

Consider: This is a way to determine if children are using magical thinking or are being practical in their choices (like getting somewhere on a magic carpet versus an airplane). Any answer is okay!

Notes:

Conundrum #73:

If you could pick one profession to do as an adult (and it has to be real – not a superhero), what would you pick to do?

Consider: Kids might not know what a profession is – and the adult can explain that it's a job that people do to earn money. There are many creative, moral, and ethical ways that people can earn money. If a child wants to do something that is ultimately low-paying or very impractical (be a professional ballplayer or the president of the United States), this is perfectly okay. Do not halter or impede the child's imagination. This is not the time to try to funnel/channel the child into some real-world practical career path.

Notes:

Conundrum #74:

If you had a voice like Ariel in the Little Mermaid or Aladdin in the movie Aladdin, would you travel around and sing? What would you do with your talent?

Consider: If a child says, "No" – then ask, "Why not?" and then "What would you rather do with your beautiful singing voice?"

Notes:

Conundrum #75:

If you found something valuable on the ground, what do you think would be the right thing to do with it?

Kids should be thinking along the lines of:

Turn it in to a trustworthy adult
Take it to the police station and turn it in

Consider: If a child says that they would keep the item, and that they truly believed that was the right thing to do, the adult should probably drop the subject and then revisit it a week or two later by giving an example such as, "Oh, look what I just found! Because I know that this isn't mine, I'm going to turn it in to the store manager (or whomever is appropriate)."

There is much value to waiting to discuss an item so that they child doesn't shut down. This is one of those times where this is just a learning experience – and the entire purpose of the

Conundrum experience is to help develop critical thinking skills in children. When an adult determines that a child is lacking a particular skill, the skill should be taught later on in a safe and quiet way. Then, a few months later, revisit the Conundrum and see if the child's answer has changed.

Notes:

Conundrum #76:

You got to make just one wish. You said, "I wish for a million bucks." Instead of getting money – all of a sudden your entire neighborhood is filled with a million male deer! What are you going to do?

Consider: Kids might need to learn that the word "buck" has a double meaning – "buck" as in "male deer" and "buck" as in dollar. The answers to this Conundrum are quite hilarious as kids talk about how they will round up the deer.

Notes:

Conundrum #77:

You wake up in the morning, and find you can fly. What are you going to do?

Variation: Would you be afraid to go very high? How high would you fly? How far?

Notes:

Conundrum #78:

You can bring to life ANY animated character from a movie. Which one would you choose to bring to life?

Extension: Your character doesn't understand real humans and is very confused. What are you going to tell him or her about living on Earth?

Notes:

Conundrum #79:

You wake up in the morning and discover you've grown one whole foot overnight – what would you do? What things would be different? How would your family react?

Notes:

Conundrum #80:

You're being babysat and the babysitter has invited a friend over and they are ignoring you completely. What do you do?

Kids should be thinking along the lines of:

- Call your mom and dad.
- Call a neighbor to come over.
- Sit quietly in your room.

Consider: Kids might say that they would take advantage of the situation and do whatever they want. This answer would require some teaching-after-the-fact (3 days to two weeks later). This is something that should be addressed, but during a safe and quiet moment.

Notes:

Conundrum #81:

How could you earn $20??? (And you can't ask anyone for the money).

Consider: This helps kids connect money with work ethic!

Notes:

Conundrum #82:

There's a new kid in your class. How could you make it so that you could be friends to them?

Kids should be thinking along the lines of:

Invite them to play with you at recess.
Invite them for an afterschool play date
Eat lunch with them
Do a school project with them
Ask the teacher if you can sit with the new kid during a project or assignment

Consider: If the child says they wouldn't make an effort, this could be a sign that the child is in a clique, or possibly that they need to develop social skills. It could also be a sign that your child has enough friends and is perfectly content with that group.

It is possible to come back later on and ask this question:

"How could someone make a new kid in school feel comfortable and welcome?"

Notes:

Conundrum #83:

Your teacher is being unfair to you. What do you do?

Kids should be thinking along the lines of:

Speak to the teacher about how you feel
Talk to your parent or other guardian
Talk to the school counselor, vice principal, principal
Try to understand both sides – take a step back and examine the situation for fairness
Do better in school – work harder

Consider: Sometimes children have the perception that a teacher is not being fair, but that's not actually true. Children sometimes view situations through a cloudy or skewed perspective. Parents or guardians, upon hearing that a teacher is "unfair" sometimes jump immediately to the conclusion that the teacher really IS unfair. This might be true, and it might not be true.

Parents should seek to gather information before dismissing a child's feelings/comments and before taking a statement at face-value and blaming a teacher.

By seeking first to understand, parents should listen actively and ask open-ended questions without being judgmental. After gathering data in a non-accusatory fashion, then parents can decide upon a course of action or inaction.

Notes:

Conundrum #84:

You really like your teacher a lot, but no one else does. What do you do about it?

Kids should be thinking along the lines of:

- Just like the teacher and don't worry about anyone else.
- Tell your friends why you like the teacher
- Don't say anything, but don't change your opinion. It's okay to like a teacher.

Notes:

Conundrum #85:

You and your friend turn around at the mall and realize your parents are not there. What do you do?

Kids should be thinking along the lines of:

- Call your parent's cell phone.
- Look for your parents.
- Go to a pre-determined meeting spot.

Notes (for #85):

Conundrum #86:

You fail a test and your teacher offers to go over it with you at lunch, but there's a big dodge ball game planned. What do you do?

Kids should be thinking along the lines of:

Go over the test at recess or after school OR just don't go to the dodge ball game.

Notes:

Conundrum #87:

You want to start a pet-sitting club. What type of pets would you pet sit? How much would you charge? Would you take care of the pets at your house or at the peoples' houses? Which of your friends would you ask to help you? How would you split the money?

Consider: These questions should be asked one at a time.

Notes:

Conundrum #88:

What do you say to a friend whom you really like who really, really, really dislikes his or her nose?

Kids should be thinking along the lines of:

- I love your nose!
- You're beautiful inside and out
- You're awesome and I wouldn't worry about it if I were you.

Notes:

Conundrum #89:

If you could invent something that could make something to eat, what would it be? How would it work? What would it look like? How much do you think it would cost at the store?

Notes:

Conundrum #90:

You have to be around a kid who has really, really bad manners for the whole weekend. What do you do?

Kids should be thinking along the lines of:
Lead by example
(Play by yourself is another option).

Notes:

Conundrum #91:

If you found the cutest little puppy wandering on shaking little legs across the road, what would you do?

Kids should be thinking along the lines of:

- Look around for the mother dog
- Take it home (until the owner can be found)
- Try to find its owner (but use caution approaching strangers)
- Contact a parent or guardian for assistance

Notes:

Conundrum #92:

You get to bring the class's snake home for the weekend – but it gets out. What would you do?

Kids should be thinking along the lines of:

- Scream bloody murder (just joking)
- Look for it
- Ask your parents and/or siblings to help you find the snake
- Tell the teacher on Monday
- Buy a replacement snake

Notes:

Conundrum #93:

Your little brother tells a whopper of a lie about flushing their parent's wedding rings down the toilet. You know the truth. What do you do?

Kids should be thinking along the lines of:

You must tell. Your brother will probably survive this.

Notes:

Conundrum #94:

Your feet have grown a lot, and you need new shoes. But your parents can't afford them. How will you get some shoes?

Kids should be thinking along the lines of:

- Go to a thrift store
- Ask neighbors if you can do small tasks for them to earn money

Note: Parents can fill in anything rational or reasonable that fits into their own socioeconomic situation – but the item needs to be something that a child MUST have (like a book for school that is required) as opposed to something a child might want (like a cool electronic game).

The key to this is to help children learn that stealing or asking someone to GIVE them something is not the best way to handle a need.   The best way is to earn an item through work.

Notes:

Conundrum #95:

You're spending the night at a friend's house and you see something that looks like a ghost. What could it really be? What would you do?

Kids should be thinking along the lines of:

- Blowing curtain
- Shadow
- An animal/pet
- Another sibling trying to spook you

What they should do:

- Wake up your friend/tell your friend
- Turn on the lights
- Grab a flashlight
- Laugh it off/tell a funny or scary story

Notes:

Conundrum #96:

You're spending the night outside in your backyard in a tent. It looks like it's going to start pouring rain. Do you stay outside? (The tent is waterproof) or would you come in? What would you do?

Consider: This is up to the children to pick, as long as they would remain warm and dry inside the tent and wouldn't be at risk of flooding.

Notes:

Conundrum #97:

You got accused of stealing a watch, but you didn't do it. What would you do?

Kids should be thinking along the lines of:

- Prove where the child was when the watch was stolen (have an alibi).
- Have them search you to prove you don't have it
- Keep calm and do not shout or cry
- Ask a trustworthy adult to come alongside and help you

Notes:

Conundrum #98:

You're making breakfast for your parents. What would you make? How would you make it? Would it be a surprise?

Consider: This is how parents can decide if kids need some cooking skills!

Notes:

Conundrum #99:

If you have to pick three presents for any three people you know what would they be, and who would you give them to?

Notes:

Conundrum #100:

If you saw a fire on your block, what would you do first? What if that didn't work? What would you do?

Kids should be thinking along the lines of:

- Immediate phone call to 911.
- Find the nearest adult
- Shout for help
- Stay away from the fire
- Use a hose on it if it is small

Notes:

Conundrum #101:

What if you were supposed to water your neighbor's lawn for vacation, but you forgot to do it. Most of the lawn turns brown and dies. What would you do to solve your problem?

Kids should be thinking along the lines of:

- Start watering immediately.
- Offer to earn the money to fix the problem.
- Apologize for your mistake.

Notes:

Conundrum #102:

If you had to help someone do one of these things, what would you pick, and why:

- Take in the groceries
- Bring in the trashcans
- Sweep the porch
- Water the lawn

Notes:

Conundrum #103:

If you had to pick ONLY one of these sports to play, what would you pick?

- Baseball
- Basketball
- Soccer
- Football
- Ice Skating
- Volleyball
- Softball

Notes:

Conundrum #104:

If you could walk to school or ride your bike to school, which would you do?

Notes:

Conundrum #105:

Which would you prefer? Playing on a swing outside, going to a park, playing with a bouncy ball, or playing with chalk? Why?

Notes:

Conundrum #106:

What is the best game system (WII, PSII, Wii, etc.)? Why?

Notes:

Conundrum #107:

What would you do if one of your favorite TV shows got cancelled?

Kids should be thinking along the lines of:

- Write a letter/e-mail to the television station
- Earn the money to purchase the series on DVD
- Find a new favorite TV show

Notes:

Conundrum #108:

Which would you rather have, the newest game system or a puppy or other animal to care for and play with?

Notes:

Conundrum #109:

You just broke your brand-new game system. What are you going to do?

Kids should be thinking along the lines of:

- See if you can fix it.
- Tell your parents
- Earn the money to have it repaired

Notes:

Conundrum #110:

Your grandparents tell you that you can pick out any one technology item. What are you going to pick?

Notes:

Conundrum #111:

You can only pick three songs to listen to on a trip. What three songs will you pick?

Notes:

Conundrum #112:

Would you rather have a laptop, an iPod, or a game system? Defend your choice.

Notes:

Conundrum #113:

You're at a gas station and your mom is filling up your car and you go into the station to buy a snack. Someone walks in who looks very suspicious. You think that maybe he is going to do something wrong. What do you do?

Kids should be thinking along the lines of:

- Immediately go back to the car.
- Tell your parent right away.

Notes:

Conundrum #114:

You're at a large amusement park. You and your friend get separated from your family. Your cell phone's battery is dead. You're waiting at the spot where you are supposed to meet if you ever get separated. A man comes up and tells you he knows where your family is. What do you do?

Kids should be thinking along the lines of:

- Never follow a stranger.
- Do not talk to the stranger.
- Look around for help from an employee at the park.
- Walk over to the park employee and ask for help.
- Always stay in a public place.

Consider: Younger kids might want to go with the stranger. This is when a parent would later on use the Story Telling or Modeling method to teach children about how to act safely.

Notes:

Conundrum #115:

You're on a bike ride with some friends and your friend does a wheelie and falls off his bike. He hits his head and is lying there without moving. You see some blood pooling around his head. You're not close to anyone's home, and neither of you have a cell phone. What do you do?

Kids should be thinking along the lines of:

- Put pressure on the wound.
- Yell for help at the same time.
- Find the closest house.
- Flag down a passing vehicle (don't get in it – have them call 911)

- Don't MOVE the friend.

Note: It is important for children to know basic first aid. Even young children should know not to move someone and to seek help immediately. They should also know how to put pressure on a wound.

Notes:

Conundrum #116:

Someone pulls over and offers you a ride home from school. What do you do and say?

Kids should be thinking along the lines of:

- Run away
- Run faster
- Yell for help while running

Notes:

Conundrum #117:

You're at a birthday party where the parents aren't home. You didn't know they weren't going to be there – they were there when you got home, and then they left. Some of you are pretty freaked out. The kid whose house it is isn't concerned at all. No one seems to be getting into any trouble at all. What do you do?

Kids should be thinking along the lines of:

Stay calm.

Call your parents

Consider: If a child is 11 or 12 years old, it's likely that kids wouldn't do anything other than just keep having fun. Teach your child to assess a situation to make sure that a situation is safe.

Notes:

Conundrum #118:

The power is off at your house and you think you hear the front door opening. You are alone with just your brothers and sisters. What do you do?

Kids should be thinking along the lines of:

Maybe it's your parents.
Look to see if it's them.
If it's not, go out a back door to a neighbor's house and ask for help.

Notes:

Conundrum #119:

You're at a friend's house and they say, "Hey – do you want to see my dad's gun collection?" What do you do? What do you say?

Kids should be thinking along the lines of:

Immediately say, "No" and leave.

Consider: This is pretty much the only correct answer. Children should literally leave the house immediately and contact their parents right away.

Notes:

Conundrum #120:

You go over to a friend's house and he takes out his dad's rifle and starts pointing it around and saying, "Bang! Bang!" What do you do?

Kids should be thinking along the lines of:

Zig-zag run out of the house immediately.
Once outside, hide behind a large tree or building.
Contact your parents.

Consider: Although parents do not wish their children to be fearful, children MUST know what to do in a situation of this nature. The only correct answer is to zig-zag run immediately out of the house and get behind a barrier and THEN figure out how to contact their parents or another trusted adult. If the child/friend comes out of the house without the gun/rifle, ask the friend to go inside and call the parents (if there is no available cell). Do not go back into the house.

Notes:

Conundrum #121:

You're walking home from the bus stop and a dog starts running and barking towards you. What do you do?

Kids should be thinking along the lines of:

- Look around for a tall object to stand on/climb
- Get behind something like a trash can or other object
- Call for help
- Grab a rock or a stick
- Shout, "Go home!" loudly or "No!" or "Sit!" (sometimes this works).

Notes:

Conundrum #122:

You see two dogs fighting across the street. What do you do?

Kids should be thinking along the lines of:

Get away from where the dogs are fighting; scream for help

Notes:

Conundrum #123:

You're walking your dog and another runs over and attacks it. Your dog is on a leash. What do you do?

Kids should be thinking along the lines of:

Let go of the leash.
Kick the other dog if it's small-ish or if you're much bigger than the dog
Yell, "Stop!"
Shout for help

Notes:

Conundrum #124:

You're at a swimming pool and people want you to go to the deep end and you're not sure you're ready. You don't want to look stupid or weak. What do you do?

Kids should be thinking along the lines of:

- Test swimming in the shallow end without touching the ground.
- Say, "Hey, Mom! Watch this!" (that way your mom is watching you carefully).
- Just be honest and say you're not sure you're up to it.
- Get out of the pool and say you're hungry (avoidance)

Notes:

Conundrum #125:

You're at a friend's pool and you dive down to pick up pennies off the deep end but you're most of the way there and think you're going to run out of air. What do you do?

Kids should be thinking along the lines of:

Turn right around and go back to the surface.

Notes:

Conundrum #126:

Your friend calls you and tells you that something bad is happening at their house. When you say you're going to tell your parents, they tell you not to tell anyone. What do you do?

Kids should be thinking along the lines of:

- Tell your parents anyway
- Ask what is happening, then tell your parents
- Tell your friend to call 911

Notes:

Conundrum #127:

You're at the ocean and get tumbled over by a wave. What do you do?

Kids should be thinking along the lines of:

- Go to the surface for air (kick off of the ground)
- Leave the water if you are hurt
- Check to see if your friends are ok

Notes:

Conundrum #128:

You find out that your friend is being left home alone after school until late in the evening. She begs you not to tell anyone, but she's still scared. What do you do?

Kids should be thinking along the lines of:

- Tell your parents
- Ask your parents if your friend can come over after school until his/her parents can pick him/her up

Notes:

Conundrum #129:

Your friend's dad gets really, really angry. Your friend likes staying at your house a lot. You just saw a pretty big bruise on his or her arm – what do you do?

Kids should be thinking along the lines of:

- Talk to your parents
- Tell a teacher
- Tell a school counselor

Notes:

Conundrum #130:

Your friend's pet has just passed away. How do you make your friend feel better? What do you say? What do you do?

Kids should be thinking along the lines of:

- Share happy memories about the pet
- Invite your friend over for a play date
- Listen if your friend wants to talk

Consider: Children can learn how to deal with grieving by helping someone else in the process of grieving. Sometimes people want to do nothing, or to ignore their friend or to change the subject. Kids can learn that it's okay to let someone talk about their pet or grieve and that eventually time will pass and individuals can move on in a healthy way.

Notes:

Conundrum #131:

You were playing with your pet and you accidentally hurt it. You feel terrible, and you're afraid your pet will die. What should you do?

Kids should be thinking along the lines of:

- Tell an adult immediately
- Do not try to move or shake the pet

Notes:

Conundrum #132:

You're playing with your dog or a friend's dog and it bites you. You don't want to tell anyone because you're afraid they'll put it to sleep. What should you do? Explain your thinking.

Kids should be thinking along the lines of:

- Asses how badly you are hurt
- If you are hurt, tell an adult

Consider: It is important children know to tell an adult, because the dog may continue to bite others. If the wound is very minor a child may not be inclined to tell.

Notes:

,

Conundrum #133:

You're moving and you find out that the place where you're moving will not take pets. You can't take your pets with you. What will you do with them?

Kids should be thinking along the lines of:

- Ask your friends and/or family members if they are able to take in your pet(s)
- Start looking for a good, safe home for your animal(s)

Notes:

Conundrum #134:

You're moving and your new apartment doesn't have a fenced yard. They say you can keep your dog there. How will you take care of your dog at the apartment?

Kids should be thinking along the lines of:

- Take the dog on many walks
- Make sure the dog goes out to go potty early in the morning, throughout the day, and right before bed
- Make sure the dog does not bark all day (as you have neighbors)
- If the dog is small, set up "wee-wee" pads

Notes:

Conundrum #135:

You see a baby locked in a car in a car seat while you're at the mall. You're with your friends. Your parents have gone ahead. What do you do?

Kids should be thinking along the lines of:

- Stay by the car and yell for help immediately
- Use your cell phone to call 911

Notes:

Conundrum #136:

You see your friend take a lip gloss or a Chapstick from the store. They tell you, "It's not even a dollar. I do it all the time." What do you do?

Kids should be thinking along the lines of:

- Tell your friend to put it back, stealing is wrong
- Tell the store manager
- Find a new friend

Notes:

Conundrum #137:

You're at the store and you're pretty sure you see a stranger slip something into his or her purse or backpack. What do you do?

Kids should be thinking along the lines of:

- Tell the cashier or a store associate
- Do NOT confront the person

Notes:

Conundrum #138:

You're at the grocery store and two strangers in front of you start a fistfight.   There's a baby sitting in their shopping cart. What do you do?

Kids should be thinking along the lines of:

- Move the shopping cart, if it's safe to do so
- Find a store associate for help

Notes:

Conundrum #139:

You're out shopping and you're finally buying a toy that you saved up for over two months. You can't wait to get it. As you walk up to the shelf, you see that there's only one left, and another kid is reaching for it. What do you do?

Kids should be thinking along the lines of:

- Ask someone working at the store if any are in the back
- Order the toy and have it shipped to your house
- Locate another store that sells the same product

Notes:

Conundrum #140:

Your friend is over spending the night and wants to watch a movie you really don't want to watch. It's not that it has a bad rating or anything like that. Actually, you've already seen it a couple of times and you just don't want to watch it again. What do you do?

Kids should be thinking along the lines of:

- Suggest another movie
- Tell your friend you've already seen it a few times
- Watch the movie again, hey at least you know you like it!

Notes:

Conundrum #141:

You get invited to dinner over at a new friend's house. Their parents are super nice, but when they bring out the dinner, every single thing that they are serving is something you hate. What do you do?

Kids should be thinking along the lines of:
- Eat the dinner anyways
- Take small bites of each item
- Smile and keep a pleasant expression on one's face while eating

Consider: Unless your child is allergic to the food, or unless there is a dietetic prerogative (such as non-Kosher foods), the child should learn that they should NEVER complain, NEVER mention it, and smile and eat the foods anyways. Being polite sometimes means eating food that is "icky" in some way.

Notes:

Conundrum #142:

You're at a slumber party for a birthday and everyone else is awake and wild and you're so tired, you can't stay awake any longer. You don't want to be the first one to sleep, so what should you do?

Kids should be thinking along the lines of:

- Go to sleep
- Try and stay up a little longer
- Wake yourself up with a cold drink

Notes:

Conundrum #143:

You're spending the night at a friend's house for the first time. It's getting late. You start to get homesick. What do you do?

Notes:

Conundrum #144:

You're spending the night at a friend's house and someone takes out some cigarettes. What do you do?

Notes:

Conundrum #145:

You're spending the night at a friend's house and your friend suggests you sneak some alcohol from the little cabinet over the stove. What do you do?

Notes:

Conundrum #146:

You want a friend to come over to your house to spend the night, but you don't really know how to ask. They've been over once or twice during the day. What do you do?

Notes (for #146):

Conundrum #147:

You invite a new friend over and they don't want to do anything you want to do. But they don't have any suggestions, either. You keep tossing out ideas and they keep getting bashed out of the water. What do you do?

Notes:

Conundrum #148:

You invite a good friend over and she says she won't come over without a third friend who is staying with her. You have nothing to do on the weekend anyways. Your mom says it's okay. You just don't know if you'll like the new friend. You've never really met before. Should you chance it?

Notes:

Conundrum #149:

You've got a friend staying with you when their parents are out of town for a week. After just a couple of days, they start to get on your nerves. Name three to five things that you could do.

Notes:

Conundrum #150:

You're walking to a friend's house for the first time by yourself and you get lost. Your cell phone has no reception. What do you do?

Notes:

Conundrum #151:

You lose your brand new favorite sweater and you have NO idea where you could have lost it. What do you do? When do you tell your mom?

Notes:

Conundrum #152:

You have an important assignment for class and you have left it at school. School is already closed for the day. What can you do?

Notes:

Conundrum #153:

You've got an assignment due tomorrow and your parents don't understand the instructions the teacher gave and neither do you. What do you do?

Notes:

Conundrum #154:

Your printer stops working with one page half way out and you've got a 3-page homework assignment that you're printing. Unfortunately, it's just 10 minutes before you have to leave for school. What do you do?

Notes:

Conundrum #155:

You don't have any Internet at your house. Your teacher keeps assigning homework that requires Internet use. What do you do?

Notes:

Conundrum #156:

The teacher asks if everyone in the class has a computer at home so that you can do assignments. No one else raises a hand to say they don't have one. You don't have a computer at home. What should you do?

Notes:

Conundrum #157:

You know your friend doesn't have a computer at home to do schoolwork. You live too far apart to share. What do you do?

Notes:

Conundrum #158:

Your teacher tells you to watch a nature show on TV that night, but you don't have TV for whatever reason. What do you do?

Notes:

Conundrum #159:

Your teacher tells you to watch a sports program on TV and write about it, but your mom forbids TV watching during the week. What do you do?

Notes:

Conundrum #160:

You've been absent from school for a week because you've been really sick. You are really far behind. How do you figure out how to catch up? What do you do?

Notes:

Conundrum #161:

You just find out that you've been invited to two birthday parties at the same time on the same day. You like both kids equally well. What do you do?

Notes:

Conundrum #162:

You find out that you've been invited to a party that your best friend hasn't been invited to. You really want to go to the party. Your best friend asks you to come over that night – she (or he) doesn't know that you've been invited. What do you say or do?

Notes:

Conundrum #163:

You need to pick a gift for a favorite adult (like your grandma), but you've only got $2.00. What could you do that is thoughtful?

Notes:

Conundrum #164:

You are outside playing and cut your hand REALLY bad. You feel dizzy and kind-of sick to your stomach. What do you do?

Notes:

Conundrum #165:

You are walking home from school and twist your ankle really, really bad. You cannot walk. You sit down on the sidewalk and take a look – it's already turning blue and swelling. What should you do?

Notes:

Conundrum #166:

You're climbing trees with a friend and you fall out. Fortunately, you can catch a branch on your way down, but you still hit pretty hard. You tried to break your fall with your left arm and you hear a snap. Now you can't move your fingers and it really, really hurts. You just sit there and cry for a while. Your friends come down and are just staring. One runs away. What do you do?

Notes:

Conundrum #167:

You are playing in the park and you see an old guy that you think may be dead. He's not moving at all. What do you do?

Notes:

Conundrum #168:

You hear gunfire while you're walking home from school. What would you do?

Notes:

Conundrum #169:

Your two best friends get into a huge fight. What do you do? What bad thing might happen next if you do that?

Notes (for #169):

Conundrum #170:

Your teacher assigns you a book to read that is *way* too hard for you. What do you do?

Notes:

Conundrum #171:

Name three absolutely free presents that you could give to other people.

Notes:

Conundrum #172:

You've read a really great book and want to give it to a friend, but you can't afford to buy another copy. Should you give away your favorite book? Or is there another solution?

Notes:

Conundrum #173:

You lose your calculator at school and two days later see a kid from another class using it. Your name was not on it. How can you prove it was yours?

Notes:

Conundrum #174:

You've just lost a tooth and can't find it (it fell out of your pocket at school). You want the tooth fairy to come. What should you do?

Notes:

Conundrum #175:

You've been working on a story for a LONG time and your computer crashes. You don't have it on backup. What do you do?

Notes:

Conundrum #176:

You have to write a report on a president for school. When you're searching on the Internet, you find a pretty good report. Should you use it and just switch it around a bit so that no one knows? No one will ever find out.

Notes:

Conundrum #177:

If you had to live with someone you really didn't like for a long time – what would you do?

Notes:

Conundrum #178:

A family relative whom you really don't know very well has gotten ill. He or she is really old anyways. Your parents are upset and keep driving a long way (with you in the car) to visit. It's keeping you from your friends, and you don't really like hanging around with someone who is sick. What should you do?

Notes:

Conundrum #179:

You've got a big baseball game the next weekend. Your brother (with whom you share a bedroom) catches the flu. You don't want to get sick. What should you do?

Notes:

Conundrum #180:

You love playing baseball, but your coach makes you sit on the bench for half of every game (or more). What can you do to get him to play you more?

Notes:

Conundrum #181:

You really, really like to play sports, but your parents don't think it's all that great. They don't really have the time to drive you to games and practices, but they aren't completely against you playing. What can you do so that you can play your sport?

Notes:

Conundrum #182:

You want to take musical instrument lessons, but there just isn't the money for it. What can you do?
Notes (for #182):

Conundrum #183:

Your teacher farts loudly in class and then looks horribly embarrassed. Everyone else laughs. What do you do?

Notes:

Conundrum #184:

You see that the principal of your school has a long strand of toilet paper dragging from the bottom of his shoe. What should you do?

Notes:

Conundrum #185:

You go into the bathroom at school and discover someone has spray-painted something bad. You turn around and see the kid – and the kid sees you. What do you do?

Notes:

Conundrum #186:

You never get a chance on the swings at recess. You really, really like to swing. What should you do?

Notes:

Conundrum #187:

You hurt your hand playing tetherball and every time you've tried to play for the last week, your hand hurts so bad you want to cry. Tetherball is your favorite game. What should you do?

Notes:

Conundrum #188:

You keep getting paired up with someone in your class who cheats. Your teacher doesn't let kids "tattle" on other kids. What should you do?

Notes:

Conundrum #189:

You absolutely hate a certain subject, and you have to study it for an hour a day at school. What do you do?

Notes:

Conundrum #190:

You are taking music lessons and you get pulled out of class once a week to go play with the orchestra. That's great and you love that. Unfortunately, it's in the middle of your favorite subject and you are starting to fall behind. What do you do?

Notes:

Conundrum #191:

You're behind in a subject and it embarrasses you. What can you do about it? What do bad students do when they are struggling at something? What do good students do when they are struggling at something?

Notes:

Conundrum #192:

Your friend confesses something to you. It's that they want to get smarter, but they think they are dumb. You know that's not true, but just saying, "You're not dumb" doesn't help. What can you do?

Notes:

Conundrum #193:

Everyone in your class can do 3 pull-ups. You can't. What do you do about it?

Notes:

Conundrum #194:

Your teacher divides up the class into groups and tells you to put on a play from a scene in a book you're all reading. One of your group members is terribly shy and doesn't want to do anything in front of the class. What do you do?

Notes:

Conundrum #195:

You're working at centers in school. You get a chance to paint something and you accidentally knock over the paint and it gets on the desk, the floor, and your clothes. What do you do?

Notes:

Conundrum #196:

One of the kids in the class barfs all over the desk next to you. What do you do?

Notes:

Conundrum #197:

There's a really nice checker at the grocery store whom you see every week. Her tummy is getting bigger and bigger and you think she may be having a baby. How do you find out if she is or not? Should you ask?

Notes:

Conundrum #198:

You're looking at a new baby and can't tell if it's a boy or a girl. What should you do?

Notes:

Conundrum #199:

You meet a pretty nice kid at school who looks different from anyone else. The other kids aren't super nice to the new kid. What do you do?

Notes:

Conundrum #200:

Your mom is forcing you to play with a kid whom you really don't like. You put up with it several times, but it's almost a nightmare to have to play with this kid. You're polite and don't want to upset anyone. What do you do?

Notes (#200):

Conundrum #201:

You are going to sing a solo in the Christmas show. You're excited and nervous, but your family is going to be there and you can't wait. You get laryngitis and can't sing that night. What do you do?

Notes:

Conundrum #202:

You have to get up on stage and take a part in a play. What are some ways that you can insure your success so that you do your very best?

Notes:

Conundrum #203:

You are at a friend's house and they start watching a movie that you know your parents wouldn't be happy if you saw it. The kid's parents don't seem to mind the movie. You're pretty sure that your parents are just overreacting. What should you do?

Notes:

Conundrum #204:

You're at a friend's house and they put in a DVD movie. In surprise, you realize that it's still showing in the theatres. It's been "pirated" (stolen). What do you do?

Notes:

Conundrum #205:

Your teacher has a party for the class and everyone is supposed to bring something. You totally forget. What do you do?

Notes:

Conundrum #206:

This kid you know just a little bit climbs over the school fence at recess and then comes back before the bell rings. What should you do?

Notes:

Conundrum #207:

You really want a toy that a kid in your class is playing with. What should you do?

Notes:

Conundrum #208:

No one seems to like you. You're lonely and want some friends. How do you find out what is keeping them away from you? Who do you ask for help or advice? Are you willing to change a bit to make friends? What are you willing to change?

Notes:

Conundrum #209:

All of the popular kids at school wear a certain type of clothes and you don't even like those clothes. Would you wear them just to hang out with the popular kids?

Notes:

Conundrum #210:

Everyone at school has seen a particular movie and is talking about it all the time. You feel left out. There is no way you're going to get to see it – at least, not until it comes out on DVD. Some kids ask you what you thought of the movie. What do you do?

Notes:

Conundrum #211:

You are going to go on an airplane for the very first time. You're excited and a little bit nervous. It's going to be a long flight (more than 5 hours). What do you bring with you?

Notes:

Conundrum #212:

You have a snuggle blanket or maybe a stuffed animal that you sleep with. Do you take it over to a friend's house? What if it could get lost or damaged? What if they make fun of you?

Notes:

Conundrum #213:

You would really like a kitten, but your parents say you're not old enough. How can you prove that you are responsible?

Notes:

Conundrum #214:

You just love horses. You read every book about them and you collect miniature horses and play with them. You've even gotten to go riding a few times. Your parents say that you will never get to own a horse. There is a stable within bike-riding distance from your home. What should you do?

Notes:

Conundrum #215:

You're playing near a river and one of your friends slips in and hits his or her head. What should you do?

Notes:

Conundrum #216:

Your friends want you to go on a ride that goes around and around, but these rides make you sick and throw up. What do you do?

Notes:

Conundrum #217:

You want to write a story, but every time you start, it just doesn't come out right. What do you do?

Notes:

Conundrum #218:

There is the bossiest girl on the playground. She's in your class, too. She tells everyone else what to do and how to do it. What do you do?

Notes:

Conundrum #219:

There's this boy who always tells you what to do. You can't stand it – you want to try stuff out on your own. You've told him this a couple of times – but he never listens. What do you do?

Notes:

Conundrum #220:

You see a kid drowning in a pool. There are no adults around. What do you do?

Secondary question: What if your cell phone doesn't work?

Notes:

Conundrum #221:

You're walking home from school and you hear a scream and a cry for help. The person sounds really scared. What do you do?

Notes:

Conundrum #222:

You find a baby bird that has fallen out of its nest. It only has a couple of feathers, and its eyes are already open. You don't see the mama bird or the papa bird. What do you do?

Notes:

Conundrum #223:

You know a kid who is really, really good at playing the piano, but who doesn't want to play in front of other people. What can you say?

Notes:

Conundrum #224:

You want to do better in a subject in school. What are three things that you can do to improve? Explain your answers and justify them. What's the best choice, then the next choice, and the third choice? Can you do all of them?

Notes:

Conundrum #225:

You are at school and the teacher says something that you absolutely positively know is not true. What do you do?

Notes:

Conundrum #226

You are at school and you hear two teachers talking and laughing about a student. You feel bad for the student and mad at the teachers. What should you do?

Notes:

Conundrum #227:

If everyone in your family got sick with the flu – but you were not – what could you do to help take care of them until they got better?

Notes:

Conundrum #228:

If you had to move to any state in the United States other than the one you live in, which state would you pick and why?

Notes:

Conundrum #229:

If you had to move to another city within your state (and not the one you live in) – where would you move, and why?

Notes:

Conundrum #230:

If you had to pick living in the desert, in the mountains, or by the ocean, where would you live and why? What type of a house would you like to live in? Describe it.

Notes:

Conundrum #231:

If you were driving with your parents in the car and you all got lost, what would you do? How could you help?

Notes:

Conundrum #232:

What do you do if some adult starts yelling at you for no reason at all? You didn't do anything wrong. Suddenly you realize they think you're someone else – they've got the wrong person. How do you calm them down and clear it up and still be respectful?

Notes:

Conundrum #233:

You watch a car back out of a driveway. It hits one of your neighborhood friends who was riding a bike. Your friend goes flying. What do you do first, second, and third?

Notes:

Conundrum #234:

The power went out in the middle of the night and no one's alarms went off. Your entire family oversleeps on an accident. Your dad will be late to work. You're going to be late to school. What can you do to hurry up? What would you do first? What would you leave out (not do?) in order to hurry? What could you do to be sure that no one is late like that again?

Notes:

Conundrum #235:

Your kid sister (or brother) keeps tattling on you and your parents ALWAYS take their side. What can you do?

Notes:

Conundrum #236:

It's a Saturday night and your mom and dad say you can stay up late and watch a movie. You're excited. But they get tired and go to bed. You look around and realize that lots of lights are on but you're all alone. You start to feel a little creepy. What can you do?

Notes:

Conundrum #237:

You know a kid at school who tells everyone his relatives are all famous people, but you know they are not. What do you do?

Notes:

Conundrum #238:

You're on a bike ride far from home and you get a flat tire. You're with two other friends. What should you do?

Notes:

Conundrum #239:

Your folks stick you with chores every week that you really don't like to do. Is there a way you can figure out to get them to switch you to different chores?

Notes:

Conundrum #240:

A friend wants to show you some gross stuff on the Internet. He (or she) doesn't tell you in advance and you actually see some of the stuff. What are you going to do?

Notes:

Conundrum #241:

People are writing terrible things about a friend on their My Space account. What are you going to do? List three possibilities.

Notes:

Conundrum #242:

You're playing a pick-up basketball game (just a bunch of people getting together to play – it's informal…no referee). One of your teammates is playing too rough because he (or she) wants to win. What would you do about it?

Notes:

Conundrum #243:

What are three toys that you could make for a kitten to safely play with?

Notes:

Conundrum #244:

Your friend tells a whopper of a lie to your teacher at school. You know the truth. The lie your friend told won't hurt anyone. What do you do?

Notes:

Conundrum #245:

You find a wrapped candy bar in the lunchroom at school. Do you eat it? Do you share it with a friend?

Secondary question: You find one (totally wrapped) on the playground. Do you eat it? Do you share it with a friend?

Notes:

Conundrum #246:

Science is everywhere. Name three normal things in your everyday life that science has helped.

Notes:

Conundrum #247:

When you plug in the toaster, bright yellow and blue sparks come out of the toaster and the plug. What do you do?

Notes:

Conundrum #248:

You need to know what the weather is going to be like tomorrow so you can go on a picnic with some friends. List two (or three) different ways you can figure out what the weather is going to be.

Notes:

Conundrum #249:

Friends tell you something terrible about something that they read on the Internet. They said there is a killer virus in the milk that everyone is drinking. You're not sure if it's really true. How are you going to check their facts?

Notes:

Conundrum #250:

Your friends tell you something awful about one of your friends. You're shocked and surprised because this particular friend is usually a great person. Your other friends might just be jealous. How are you going to check the facts of the story without embarrassing anyone?

Notes:

Conundrum #251:

You tried to complete a big project. You worked hard on it, but it wasn't as successful as you wanted. How do you deal with the disappointment?

Notes:

Conundrum #252:

You realize that the part in the play that you tried out for and got is much bigger than you thought it was going to be. You think that maybe you've bitten off more than you can chew. What do you do?

Notes:

Conundrum #253:

You're painting something in your bedroom and a big blob of paint drops onto the carpet. What are the first three things you do?

Notes (for #253):

Conundrum #254:

You have a fear of public speaking and you have to read a presentation in front of the class. What are steps you can take to conquer your fear?

Notes:

Conundrum #255:

You're going to your friend's house and he invites another person that you don't like over. They don't pay any attention to you at all and only play together. What do you do?

Notes:

Conundrum #256:

You are at a duck pond feeding the ducks and you see a kid fall in and go in over his head. What do you do?

Notes:

Conundrum #257:

It's only 3 days to your mother's birthday and you need to get her a present. You don't have any money. What do you do?

Notes:

Conundrum #258:

You borrow $5 from someone you know to buy something really cool that you wanted. But it was a mistake because you have no way to pay it back. What are you going to do?

Notes:

Conundrum #259:

You are playing outside and you break a piece of city property. Who can you tell? How can you help get this fixed?

Notes:

Conundrum #260:

You borrow your friend's skateboard and you lose it. Do you tell him? What do you do?

Notes:

Conundrum #261:

You do a job for someone and they don't pay you as much as they promised. You were going to get $10.00 and they only give you $5.00. What do you do?

Notes:

Conundrum #262:

What are three simple things you can do to help other people in your community?

Notes:

Conundrum #263:

You make up your mind to have a wonderful day. You help out three students at your school. What three things are you going to do?

Notes:

Conundrum #264:

You and a friend decide to pick up trash to clean up your neighborhood and do a good deed. What supplies will you need? What things will you need to consider?

Notes:

Conundrum #265:

You and three friends decide to paint a neighbor's white picket fence. The neighbor is handicapped and can't do it alone. He has the paint for you to use. You've got permission from your parents. What other supplies and tools do you need? What will you need to think about (what could go wrong so that you don't make a mess of the job)?

Notes:

Conundrum #266:

You want to help someone secretly. They can never find out.

1)   If it's for an adult in your neighborhood, what could you do?   What do you need to consider to stay safe?

2)   If it's for a kid at your school, what could you do?

Notes:

Conundrum #267:

You're raising money for your school. You go out in pairs together just like your school instructions said, and a nice old lady wants to invite you inside. What do you do? What do you say?

Notes:

Conundrum #268:

You see a classmate who is struggling academically. You believe you might be able to help. How can you help out and still preserve their dignity so that they won't feel embarrassed?

Notes:

Conundrum #269:

You hear what sounds like a loud explosion down the street. Your parents are home, but sleeping. What should you do?

Notes:

Conundrum #270:

What could you do today to make the world a better place?

Notes:

Conundrum #271:

You're out hiking in the woods. You get separated from your family and shouting out loud isn't helping. No one seems to know where you are. You try to find your way back, but you can't. It's starting to get dark and the temperature is dropping. What do you do?

Notes (#271):

Conundrum #272:

You find a wounded wild raccoon while out on a nature hike. It's awake, but bleeding pretty badly. What do you do?

Notes:

Conundrum #273:

You're visiting the woods on vacation and you got to bring a friend with you. It started raining and kept pouring for two whole days. Finally the sun comes out and you can go out to play. Your folks say you can go out. Your friend wants to go play by the river, but it's swollen and rushing with water. What should you do?

Notes:

Conundrum #274:

You love nature and the outdoors and have been camping several times. You are playing "camping" at home and you want to build a fire to make it real. How should you go about this?

Notes:

Conundrum #275:

If you go on a nature hike, what things should you take with you in order to stay safe?

Notes:

Conundrum #276:

If you go on a nature hike, what things should you not touch or do in order to stay safe? List at least 3 things and explain why.

Notes:

Conundrum #277:

How do you know when it's time to come in outside from playing? List three times when you should go indoors.

Notes:

Conundrum #278:

Your parents tell you they're tired of you hanging out inside and tell you to go outside to play. List five fun things you can do safely outside.

Notes:

Conundrum #279:

Your little brother says there's a monster in his closet. What do you do to help him figure out it's not real?

Notes:

Conundrum #280:

You are feeling depressed or sad. What positive steps can you take to help feel better? List at least 3 steps.

Notes:

Conundrum #281:

Your mom comes home from work and she's really tired. Grouchy, too. What can you do to help out around the house so she can rest quietly for a little while?

Notes:

Conundrum #282:

What are three foods that you can avoid or quit eating so that you are a healthy eater?

Notes:

Conundrum #283:

Your parents want you to eat healthier. You like what you eat now! Still, you want to make some changes because you love your folks, so what two healthy foods will you add in to your weekly diet and what two unhealthy foods will you cut out?

Notes:

Conundrum #284:

List three unhealthy ingredients commonly found in packaged foods. How do you find out if something isn't good for you? What do you do to not eat those ingredients?

Notes:

Conundrum #285:

List five healthy foods that you already eat and enjoy.

Notes:

Conundrum #286:

Describe the best things about your personality. You can't list anything that you look like. List at least 4 positive things.

Notes:

Conundrum #287:

What is one thing that you'd like to change about yourself that you really can change right away?

Notes:

Conundrum #288:

What do you do if you want to change something about yourself? For example, what if you catch yourself lying all the time and you don't like that about yourself. What are you going to do to stop it?

Notes:

Conundrum #289:

Everybody is good at something. What are you good at? List at least 3 things.

Notes:

Conundrum #290:

You have to share your funniest moment at school. But you can't think of anything funny you've ever done. What should you do?

Notes:

Conundrum #291:

You've always been really good at something (like painting or reading or singing or sports or cooking…that sort of stuff), and all of a sudden you've hit a roadblock. The project you're working on (like a picture or a book or a song, etc) is really hard and you're not sure if you can do it well. What do you do?

Notes:

Conundrum #292:

Everyone around you seems to be able to jump rope pretty well. You don't do it very well. What steps can you take to get better at it?

Notes:

Conundrum #293:

You accidentally super-glue something to the kitchen table. Basically, you're going to be busted. What are you going to do?

Notes:

Conundrum #294:

People who are the best at things (like sports stars, mathematicians, chess players, singers, artists, dancers, or scientists...) work very, very hard to get where they are going. They often have many obstacles along the way that they must overcome – some of them very challenging. Pick one thing that you might want to be when you grow up and list three obstacles that you might have to overcome. Why would you decide to keep going instead of quit?

Notes:

Conundrum #295:

Why do some people quit at hard things while other people keep going when they get to a similar hard thing?

Notes:

Conundrum #296:

What makes a person a quitter?

Secondary Question: What makes a person a success in spite of encountering difficulties?

Notes:

Conundrum #297:

If you could travel by supersonic jet airplane, space ship, luxury cruise ship, or a blimp – which would you choose and why? If you had to put these in order, what's the first one you'd pick and the second and so forth.

Notes:

Conundrum #298:

If you could go to any amusement park in the world and stay for a whole week, where would you go?

Notes:

Conundrum #299:

What person from history would you really like to talk to? What one or two questions would you ask (they have to tell you the truth – that's a part of the "Rules" of this conundrum).

Notes:

Conundrum #300:

You're doing an assignment on the computer and the power pops off for a minute. What should you do? You did press save, but several minutes ago.

Notes:

Conundrum #301:

You're having trouble remembering to turn in your homework. You always do it – it's just that you forget to bring it or turn it in. What should you do to help yourself remember?

Notes:

Conundrum #302:

You have to do the laundry for the first time. Say out loud the steps that you need to take to do the wash in a washing machine and dryer.

Notes:

Conundrum #303:

You want to cook scrambled eggs. What are the steps that you need to take to cook it and clean up afterward?

Notes:

Conundrum #304:

You're going to make a salad. What would you put in it?

Notes:

Conundrum #305:

List three easy desserts that you can make with just a little help. Why did you pick these?

Notes:

Conundrum #306:

You want to make brownies, but you've never done it before. Your dad is home, but he's busy. Still – he says that you can try. How do you go about figuring out how to make brownies?

Notes:

Conundrum #307:

It's Mother's Day tomorrow. What three things are you going to do for your mom?

Notes:

Conundrum #308:

It's Father's Day tomorrow. What three things are you going to do for your dad?

Notes:

Conundrum #309:

Your grandma is coming over to visit. What four things can you do to make her feel special?

Notes:

Conundrum #310:

You lose some of the pieces of your favorite game. What can you do to solve this problem?

Notes:

Conundrum #311:

You've looked around and have noticed that some of the kids who are "popular" are pretty nasty people – and some of them make bad choices. You want to have a lot of friends, but you don't want to fall into that trap of being unkind to others. What are some things that you can do to make friends and still feel good about yourself?

Notes:

Conundrum #312:

You are given a choice at school. Would you rather have indoor recess or outdoor recess and what would you do?

Notes:

Conundrum #313:

You have to earn some money to buy something you want. What house chores would you do to choose it?

Some examples:
Water the garden - Empty the trashcans - Sweep the floors

Notes:

Conundrum #314:

You have a choice to either go to a friend's house or see a movie with your family. Which would you do?

Notes:

Conundrum #315:

You get to redo your room. Would you rather use a favorite color or a favorite theme (like a TV show or movie or sport?)

Notes:

Conundrum #316:

You're at school. You're going to write book report. Would you rather pick fiction or non-fiction?

Notes:

Conundrum #317:

You get to pick your book to read. Would you rather pick a long one or a short one, and why?

Notes:

Conundrum #318:

If you couldn't play anything electronic for the day, would you rather play mostly indoors, or mostly outdoors?

Notes:

Conundrum #319:

You're going shopping. Would you rather pick a clothing item or a game?

Secondary Question: Now list what you'd get – but it can just be one thing and only for _____ dollars (parents or teachers – fill in any amount you'd like.)

Notes:

Conundrum #320:

It's your birthday party. Would you rather have it a class party or have just a couple of friends?

Notes:

Conundrum #321:

You're picking out a kitten for a pet. Would you rather have one with long hair or short hair? Explain your thinking.

Secondary question: Does the color of the kitten matter to you? Why or why not?

Notes:

Conundrum #322:

It's a family member's birthday. Would you rather make them breakfast in bed or dinner that evening?

Notes:

Conundrum #323:

You get to pick a family vacation. Would you rather go somewhere warm and tropical (the beach) or would you rather go somewhere where there is snow for sledding?

Notes:

Conundrum #324:

If you were a super hero would you rather have super strength or the ability to fly?

Secondary Question: Or is there some other super power that you would rather have?

Notes:

Conundrum #325:

It's the first day of school. Do you want to sit at the front of the classroom or the back of the classroom? Why?

Notes:

Index

Contact Us:

We love to hear from you! If you have any situations you'd like to see in future books, send us an e-mail. We love to hear feedback, and we'd love to put in your testimonial into future editions of Conundrum Kids.

Contact us at:

Conundrumkidsnow@gmail.com

AlisaGriffis.com

Like us on FaceBook: **Conundrum Kids**

Coming Soon!

Conundrum Kids 2 – 325 more conundrums for 5-12 year olds designed to give parents and teachers even more opportunities to develop solid critical thinking skills within children!

Conundrum Kids: Entrepreneur!
Conundrums for kids who'd like to get some experience working – and earning money! This book is designed to help kids start their own business – and "pre disaster" them in the process: When kids think about potential pitfalls in advance, they can strategize and make better choices for their present.

Conundrum Kids: Youth Group edition: Christian conundrums designed to help youth groups and home schooling families instill a love of Christ into their children.

16195866R00090

Made in the USA
San Bernardino, CA
22 October 2014